Terms of Survival

Poems by

Judith Ortiz Cofer

Arte Público Press
Houston, Texas
1995

Acknowledgment is made to the following publications for poems that originally appeared in them: *Cotton Boll: The Atlanta Review, Palmetto Review, Passages North, Revista Chicano-Riqueña, South Carolina Review, Southern Exposure, Woman of Her Word: Hispanic Women Write*. A number of these poems have also appeared in two earlier chapbooks: *Peregrina* (Riverstone Press) and *The Native Dancer* (Pteranodon Press).

I would like to thank the Virginia Center for the Creative Arts, where most of these poems were written during a residency.

*PS
3565
.R7737
T4
1995*

This book has been made possible by a grant from the National Endowment for the Arts, a federal agency.

Recovering the past, creating the future

Arte Público Press
University of Houston
Houston, TX 77204-2090

ISBN 1-55885-079-1
LC 87-070270

Second Edition, 1995
Printed in the United States of America

Contents

I. Palabras

II. Common Ground

Terms of Survival is dedicated to the
memory of my father,
J. M. Ortiz Lugo

Terms of Survival

Palabras

Polonius: *What do you read, my lord?*
Hamlet: *Words, words, words.*

Hamlet, II, ii, 195

Quinceañera

My dolls have been put away
like dead children, in a chest
I will carry with me when I marry.
I reach under my skirt
to feel a satin slip bought for this day.
It is soft as the inside of my thighs.
My hair has been nailed back
with my mother's black hairpins to my skull.
Her hands stretched my eyes open
as she twisted braids
into a tight circle
at the nape of my neck.
I am to wash my own clothes and sheets
from this day on,
as if the fluids of my body were poison,
as if the little trickle of blood
I believe travels from my heart to the world
were shameful.
Is not the blood of saints
and men in battle beautiful?
Do Christ's hands
not bleed into your eyes
from His cross?
At night
I hear myself growing
and wake to find my hands
drifting of their own will
to soothe skin stretched tight
over my bones.
I am wound like the guts of a clock,
waiting for each hour to release me.

San Antonio al Revés

You are the patron saint
of women who wait
lighting candles at your feet,
San Antonio,
every Saturday morning and night,
that you intercede for them
in God's blue heaven,
and save their sons and husbands
from the rum-slick bodies of *putas*,
and deliver them
from the blades of drunken friends.
Virgins
stand you on your blessed head,
San Antonio al revés,
for luck, promising hymens
as dowry, and their prayers
are like an extra blanket
at the foot of their winter beds,
San Antonio, San Antonio al revés.

La Envidia

It is a green snake:
the fashionable necklace
your best friend wears,
the fat red cheeks
of someone else's baby,
the man with muscles
like twisted rope
whose arms
will never circle your waist,
 your mother's breasts
you remember
as ripe fruit she saved
for the next child and the next.
It is the flight of migrating birds
you watch from your room every autumn,
heading for islands
where wishes grow like coconuts
on beaches you will never see.

La Fe

When the bells peal in octaves
in my head,
I fight the urge to genuflect
before marble statues,
to light candles
in colors to saints.
I breathe a litany
to save the day.
Each night
as I kiss the cross
I pray
to be released from rituals.

La Maldad

It is the evil eye.
The fate your enemy quickens
with a curse,
the poison of an invisible dart
that twists a fetus into a monster,
that drives a lover away,
crossing the paths of desire,
so that he never returns to your bed.
Only a strong amulet of black onyx
worn around the neck or wrist
on a gold chain
can defeat *la maldad*,
by absorbing evil like a leech,
until it bursts.

Loca

When she closes her eyes,
the world empties from her head
like oil through a funnel.
Under the clear blue canopy
of her fantasy, she invents
new sounds for a tongue
all her own, and colors
so pure she must spend hours
holding on to each hue.
So far has she gone
into herself,
that the taunting voices
from the outside calling
her, *Loca*, *Loca*,
reach her as bright beams
of light lining the road
to the kingdom where
she is the sole ruler.

Judith Ortiz Cofer

Las Malas Lenguas

It happened to the plump fair daughter
of an honest *campesino*,
who was caught on her knees pledging her soul
and her body to the devil.
Nothing could save her from the acid
of her neighbors' tongues,
or her father's curse, *maldita seas*.
She grew old quickly, and went mad.
They say her demon lover's cloven prints
can still be seen on that pasture by moonlight,
así dicen las malas lenguas.

Siempre

A lover's word.
On tombstones it is a plea
for remembrance.
The little immortality.
The rough measure
of infinity calculated by
the heart's liquid clock.

Nunca

It is a bullet caught in bone.
A gavel striking the judge's bench.
It is a rock falling in the night,
on the tin roof of the house
you can never again enter.
It is the final click
of brass handles on a coffin.
A shovel hitting rock.

El Mal

Le hizo el mal,
I heard my mother say
about a girl we were
no longer allowed to see.
It sounded like a spell.
In my naiveté, I imagined
a witch preparing a brew
to poison my fair friend
out of spite,
for her beauty.
But fairy tales could not explain
the swelling belly or
the hurry-up wedding.
El Mal, I have since learned,
is an old sorcerer's trick that begins
by mixing man, woman and moon.

La Vida

Everyone and everything
was reflected
on the shiny black
patent leather purse
Virgilia carried on her arm
from campo to town
like a Roman shield.
What went into it
was a night's wages,
warm from the pockets
of the laborers who paid
for the oblivion
of her noncommittal flesh.
Vessel or oracle:
they all became penitents
at the altar of her thighs,
columns on a pagan temple.
Like the communal well,
Virgilia carried within her
all the secret wishes
that can be made
with the toss of a coin.

Judith Ortiz Cofer

Costumbre

In Old San Juan
prostitutes play
dominoes
in the public square
with men,
and the wives
who must walk by
on their way
to evening mass
cross themselves
and look away.

Caminante

I have a sky inside my head
and I was born to follow my own shadow
drifting like a cloud.
I sleep where I sit,
in trains screaming through the snow,
or in the back of a flatbed truck,
where a man can go blind
looking up into the sun.
It makes me melancholy to see
old women in heavy black
walking on the shoulders of dangerous roads.
Sometimes I want to jump down
like some ragged angel
scorched from flying too close to the sun,
and offer myself to them, saying:
I will be as a son to you.
Other times, my heart breaks free
when I look upon a field plowed in lines
to the edge of the horizon.

Judith Ortiz Cofer

Esperanza

My name mocks me
for I was born at the cost
of my mother's life,
earning my father's hatred
with my first breath.
All my life
I have scoured a house
soiled with the thick soot
of his resentment.
It has left its mark
on the walls,
in his eyes,
and on me.
All of it
I have tried to wipe away.
In my hands
I hold a broom;
in my heart—
ashes, ashes.

El Encanto

I shape the wax
into a hand-sized you
and let it melt all night.
I burn pyramids of patchouli
until my eyes water.
Tonight the moon begins to wane,
y ni la más poderosa magia
will prevail in the darkness
that will follow.
My candle will burn in a vacuum.
Reaching for you
across time and distance,
your image will elude me
like the most cryptic of spells.

Judith Ortiz Cofer

La Bruja

Her face is brown and creased
like ripples on a muddy pond.
Only her eyes are alive
like those ancient nameless things
on the underside of rocks.
They say she has the power
to give life and to take it away,
that if she spits
in the path
of her enemy,
the earth will
open at his feet
like a hungry mouth;
but if she blesses a man,
he will meet death like a lover
in his own bed, in his own time.
They say she's lived a thousand lives,
consorted with both Satan and God,
so that it is always best
to avoid her consuming gaze.

Socorro

When they run past the stand
where she sells flowers,
the school children call out her name
as if they were drowning.
She is scorned by the shopkeepers
who say she sells *flores para los muertos*
and the smell of decay is driving
their customers away. She has survived
her only child. For a living
she grows chrysanthemums
on a little plot of earth
next to her house.
She talks each plant into radiance,
patting the warm soil around them
like a favorite grandchild.
And if the odor of death
clings to Socorro
it is because he is a gentleman,
who takes her elbow
when she crosses the street
each morning, and lingers
in her corner,
smelling her flowers,
waiting.

Judith Ortiz Cofer

Muerto

Muerto
is a wilting word:
It spells death, decay
and the collapse of flesh.
Muerto
is gummy and limp
like a leaf held too long
in your palm.
Muerto
is a body marked CONDEMNED—
eyes boarded up
and a tongueless mouth
like a door ajar
in an abandoned building.
Muerto.
The word rolls forward on your palate,
then back, jerks your jaw down,
forcing your mouth to circle a moan:
O, O, O. Muerto.

Día de los Muertos

In the campos,
where the rains are bringing
the feet of the living
closer to their restless bones,
the dead strain
against the creaking lids
of their mahogany coffins:
they are trying to get our attention.
The newly dead with throat and lip
moan for our benefit,
though they are in no pain.
They know
there is no turning back,
but the deceased acknowledge
no rules. They hate the living
without exception,
forgetting bonds of blood and friendship.
They envy us our breath.
But the dead too have holidays.
When we turn our heads heavenward
like turkeys in the rain, lighting candles,
telegraphing prayers, we feel generous
as the wife who sends her man
in prison a cake, while
in the soggy ground, the dead
warm their dripping bones
over the little flame
of our fears.

Judith Ortiz Cofer

Yerbatero

He believes
the earth brews
all the medicine
man needs
in her belly,
and plants send their roots
down to the boiling core
where God experiments.
Yerba buena, yerba mala,
todo se cura con la fe
y la naturaleza.

Estigmas

At first it is the sharp pain
like a knife on her right side
making her curl like a fetus
deep into her bed.
Then the purple spots on her wrists—
tender to the touch, and liquid
under the skin. Joined in prayer,
they match.
Some nights the pain lifts her
like the arms of a lover,
to the porcelain sink,
wher her blood
becomes the beads on a red rosary
she says over and over.

Judith Ortiz Cofer

Cada Día

Padre, who sits on a cloud,
danos el pan de cada día,
Madre, who stands on his left
and just a little behind,
ruega por nosotros,
Hijo Santo, de ojos azules y
corazón sangrante y grande,
listen to the pleas
of the little live things
crawling on this planet
given to you for Christmas.
Please do not toss us
into a dark corner
of your vast universe
and forget us.

Pescador

to the fishermen in Boquerón, Puerto Rico

After a day of tilting horizons,
he drags his net to the beach.
It is heavy as a lifetime of sins.
Living with the sea is not easy.
She is a demanding *querida*, a mistress
who yields herself reluctantly, and only
if won with gifts and poetry.
He must give her his constant attention,
never questioning her ways.
He knows that as he rides her currents,
she owns him—that a pescador
must always be the patient, coaxing lover,
taking from her only
what she knows he needs.

Judith Ortiz Cofer

Origen

What we want to know:
in that unimaginable moment,
the union of parental flesh,
was there love, or
are we the heirs of carelessness?
This matters.
That we were wanted, called forth
to fulfill a wish.
That we were meant to be.

Madrina: The Infant's Voice

Who is this woman
who looks at me with mother-eyes,
holding me with such certainty
in her cool arms; and why
do I fear the floating fog
of Limbo when I am pressed
to this hard empty breast
that makes me scream
with hunger and frustration?

Judith Ortiz Cofer

La Abuela

La Abuela bore twelve children;
six stayed only long enough to be named.
And each little coffin pulled her
closer to the ground.
Burdened with the weight
of all those unfinished lives, her body
carried her like a weary beast of burden
to the trough of her old age.
La Abuela then blinked out of her mourning.
She wears a pink gown now,
and sits in her rocking chair all day.

Vestido de Novia

Eyelets, cheap lace, and puffed sleeves,
bought hastily in '51
for a weekend Navy-leave *boda*.
I find it limp and yellow
on the bottom of an old cardboard trunk
she'd once called a hope chest.
I bleach it in my sink, and on the clothesline
it comes to life, tugging at the pins,
filling out with thighs and arms of breeze:
It is my mother, pale with anxiety—it is she,
trembling at the dock that Monday morning,
saying the first of a thousand goodbyes.

Judith Ortiz Cofer

Matrimonio

Here we stand at the altar,
like the penitent Adam and Eve
clothed in new religion.
The priest tells us
we are made of the same clay.
y yo digo quizás, quizás,
but molded by a nervous hand.
We are more like the snake,
shedding old skin for new.
Nature commands and we go along,
learning where we are going
as we go.

Felicia

I arrive in the late afternoon
of a perfect summer day
at the neat little house
on its green lawn island.
Inside she is preparing for my visit,
laying a clean cloth
on the dinner table,
like the women did
on that afternoon
so many years ago
when her arrival
caught us all by surprise.
I remember
mother gasping for breath,
and the thick silence in the room
as she said to me: *your sister came,
but did not stay.* For years
I wondered
if she would come back another time.
Even now, I sometimes dream
of a house where I am always expected
by my mother's other daughter, the one
we had already named Felicia.

Judith Ortiz Cofer

So Much for Mañana

After twenty years in the mainland
Mother's gone back to the Island
to let her skin
melt from her bones
under her native sun.
She no longer wears stockings,
girdles or tight clothing.
Brown as a coconut,
she takes siestas in a hammock,
and writes me letters that say:
"Stop chasing your own shadow, *niña*
come down here and taste the *piña*
put away those heavy books,
don't you worry about your shape,
here on the Island men look
for women who can carry a little weight.
On every holy day,
I burn candles and I pray
that your brain won't split
like an avocado pit
from all that studying.
What do you say?
Abrazos from your Mamá and a blessing
from that saint, Don Antonio, *el cura*."
I write back: "Someday I will go back
to your Island and get fat,
but not now, Mamá, maybe *mañana*."

Sueños

mi pie de arena y mi cabeza de astros

Luis Palés Matos

A delicate plant
requiring rich, dark soil.
If potted, place in full sunlight
and water frequently.
Without proper tending
it will fade to yellow
and the roots will become
dry and brittle.
It may react adversely
to sudden abundance:
Feed in moderation.
If this plant
is to achieve harmony
with its environment,
it must be cultivated in soil
rich with memory and choice,
and tended with hands
warmed in sunlight.

Judith Ortiz Cofer

Acróbata

Vamos, acróbatas modernos,
sobre trapecio de metáforas
a hacer maromas peligrosas
para que el gran público aplauda.

Luis Palés Matos

To him there is no greater joy
than the perfect somersault.
He lives for the stretching of tendons
to the tautness of violin strings,
and the spring of his body
toward the twin moons
of the spotlights pulling the crowds
up by their eyes.
As the coiled snake inside him
catapults him higher
than they dreamed
a man could rise,
they hold their breath,
thrusting up octopus arms
to try to touch him.
Suspended by their collective will,
he senses their excitement
building like a woman's orgasm.
Calling him by name,
they pull him down,
and he falls
weightless as a leaf
into the net of their applause.

El Error

My dead father says to me,
Es un error, un error, hija,
and I alone survived to tell you.
Sometimes his voice echoes
as if he were in a cave,
Judith, Judith, he shakes his head
in the shadows, pitying me for my doubts.
Other times he just walks in
looking younger in every dream.
Dressed in a starched *guayabera*, perfumed,
he does not remember the rain-slick road, the blood,
or being pulled from his Volkswagen
with a crowbar, extracted
like an old tooth from a gaping red mouth.

Judith Ortiz Cofer

Mamacita

Mamacita hummed all day long
over the caboose kitchen
of our railroad flat.
From my room I'd hear her *humm*,
crossing her path, I'd catch her *umm*.
No words slowed the flow
of Mamacita's soulful sounds;
it was *humm* over the yellow rice,
and *umm* over the black beans.
Up and down two syllables she'd climb
and slide—each note a task accomplished.
From chore to chore, she was the prima donna
in her daily operetta.
Mamacita's wordless song was her connection
to the oversoul,
her link with life,
her mantra,
a lifeline to her own Laughing Buddha,
as she dragged her broom
across a lifetime of linoleum floors.

La Libertad

In a hot country where cement sweats,
and the thirsty ground opens in a thousand mouths
pleading to the sky, a man waits.
Standing between bars of sunlight and shadow,
he cups a burning match to the cigarette in his mouth.
He has had time to study the gestures of patience.
He has been silenced by his own words
splattered on walls in the blood of his companions.
Now he waits for the words written in ink
that will let him walk again under the sky.
The smoke he exhales slips through the bars
like a soul from a body,
and it is enough to know that some things
cannot be taken from a man.

Judith Ortiz Cofer

El Olvido

It is a dangerous thing
to forget the climate of your birthplace,
to choke out the voices of dead relatives
when in dreams they call you
by your secret name.
It is dangerous
to spurn the clothes you were born to wear
for the sake of fashion; dangerous
to use weapons and sharp instruments
you are not familiar with; dangerous
to disdain the plaster saints
before which your mother kneels
praying with embarrassing fervor
that you survive in the place you have chosen to live:
a bare, cold room with no pictures on the walls,
a forgetting place where she fears you will die
of loneliness and exposure.
Jesús, María, y José, she says,
el olvido is a dangerous thing.

Common Ground

For time is the longest distance between two places.

Tennessee Williams, *The Glass Menagerie*, sc. vii

Common Ground

Blood tells the story of your life
in heartbeats as you live it;
bones speak in the language
of death, and flesh thins
with age when up
through your pores rises
the stuff of your origin.

These days,
when I look in the mirror I see
my grandmother's stern lips
speaking in parentheses at the corners
of my mouth of pain and deprivation
I have never known. I recognize
my father's brows arching in disdain
over the objects of my vanity, my mother's
nervous hands smoothing lines
just appearing on my skin,
like arrows pointing downward
to our common ground.

Exile

I left my home behind me
but my past clings to my fingers
so that every word I write
bears the mark
like a cancelled postage stamp
of my birthplace.
There was no anger to warn me
of the dangers of looking back.
Like Lot's wife, I would trade
my living blood for one last look
at the house where each window
held a face framed as in a family album.
And the plaza lined with palms
where my friends and I strolled
in our pink and yellow and white Sunday dresses,
dreaming of husbands, houses, and orchards
where our children would play
in the leisurely summer of our future.
Gladly would I spill my remaining years
like salt upon the ground,
to gaze again on the fishermen of the bay
dragging their catch in nets
glittering like pirate gold, to the shore.
Nothing remains of that world, I hear,
but the skeletons of houses,
all colors bled from the fabric
of those who stayed behind,
inhabiting the dead cities
like the shadows of Hiroshima.

Judith Ortiz Cofer

Under The Knife

My aunt wipes blood from her knife
across a kitchen towel, spilling
the thick contents
of a just decapitated hen into the sink.
I feel slightly nauseated but must
forbear for her sake. Childless
family martyr, renowned for her patience
with human frailty, and her cooking.
Her man drinks, she has failed three times
at childbearing. She squeezes the last
of the blood from the neck and a blue button
falls into her hand. Rinsing it, she drops it
into her apron pocket. And as she places
the pale carcass and the knife before me,
she explains how to cut the pieces, with even,
    forceful strokes:
no hacking.
She is under no obligation to be kind.
The mothers and the daughters
have given her a lifetime license
to mourn, and like a queen in exile
she acknowledges nothing as a privilege.
The pale fingers of my aunt
work with precision over the pink flesh,
showing me just how to separate
the tough from the tender.

The Course of Winds

The last place he called home
was so close to the equator
women hung their laundry on it,
long-limbed women who blossomed
fast as hothouse flowers
in the fever of the tropics.
But he had played the pale, exotic fish
snarled in seaweed hair
for long enough.
After a year of mornings in the sun
with the iguanas, letting the slow poison
of nights drain from the pores,
of smelling the simmering compost
of vegetal life, and the pungent scent
of his own immobility, he set sail
for cooler climates.
He thought in Maine nothing would spoil,
but the cool white moon
looked down on him
like his first grade teacher,
and the rocky beach
was braille to his feet:
it said, *keep walking*,
and he did.

Judith Ortiz Cofer

Past the weathered houses
crouched by the sea like retirees,
past the public buildings
where men gather
to trace the course of winds,
and down the road that leads
into landlocked America.
Now he is always on the move,
making tracks
across the inevitable state
that is always between him
and somewhere else.

Lost Relatives

In the great diaspora
of our chromosomes,
we've lost track of one another.
Living our separate lives,
unaware of the alliance of our flesh,
we have, at times, recognized our kinship
through the printed word:
Classifieds, where we trade our lives
in two inch columns;
Personals, straining our bloodlines
with our lonely hearts; and *Obituaries*,
announcing a vacancy
in our family history
through names that call us home
with their familiar syllables.

Judith Ortiz Cofer

Night Driving

The white mile markers
make me think of nuns
buried on foreign soil.
It takes a heart
larger than my chest contains
to die for bloody causes.
It's easy to admit cowardice
while driving at night alone
on a road you hope
is faithful to your memory.
The game is: what will you die for?
Though everyone I've ever said
"I love you" to, takes a number,
the final tally is woefully short.
My child dangles from the edge
of a ravine I've conjured,
with almost no hesitation
I extend my body like a bridge
over infinity.
The other voices fade
as I drive deeper into the night,
until they are no more
than the little wail of the wind.

Severance

I'm chewing away at my past
like a creature caught
in a steel trap,
spitting out gristle and blood,
waiting for the time
when pain will become habit,
or lift like a thick fog.
And when the flesh draws tight
over my wounds,
I will walk away on my own,
phantom-footed and free.

To My Father

Who died thinking himself a burden
and unloved, whose fine hands grew
too rough and calloused to hold
a pen or brush, or a child's hand.
Folded over his chest in death,
the bruised fingers would not divulge
any more than we already knew,
that this man had earned his rest.
Stubborn sentinels of his heart,
they said nothing of the silence that he built
layer by layer,
sealing himself in the place
where he kept his private grief,
or that long ago
when hope still came in and out
of our house like a cat
rubbing its head on our legs,
he had written love letters to each of us,
but perhaps afraid
that words would betray him,
he had hidden them
among the still life of rusting tools,
where I find them,
yellow and fragile
as unearthed bones, or relics.

The Idea of Islands

The place where I was born,
that mote in a cartographer's eye,
interests you?
Today Atlanta is like a port city
enveloped in mist. The temperature
is plunging with the abandon
of a woman rushing to a rendezvous.
Since you ask, things were simpler
on the island. Food and shelter
were never the problem. Most days,
a hat and a watchful eye were all
one needed for protection, the climate being
rarely inclement. Fruit could be plucked
from trees languishing under the weight
of their own fecundity. The thick sea
spewed out fish that crawled into the pots
of women whose main occupation was to dress
each other's manes with the scarlet hibiscus,
which as you may know, blooms
without restraint in the tropics.
I was always the ambitious one, overdressed
by my neighbors' standards, and unwilling
to eat mangoes three times a day.
In truth, I confess to spending my youth
guarding the fire by the beach, waiting
to be rescued from the futile round
of paradisiacal life.
How do I like the big city?

Judith Ortiz Cofer

City lights are just as bright
as the stars that enticed me then;
the traffic ebbs and rises like the tides,
and in a crowd,
everyone is an island.

Rosa

Rosa is nothing like a rose,
her flowering gone to fat
where for years the firm layers
of her flesh had contained
a dream like a pearl:
that she would one day
buy her way out of the barrio
with its rows of grey buildings
all the same,
and the cycle of poverty
that spun her playmates
into too soon weddings
with each year
the frenzy of cheap organdy gowns
cut from the same Simplicity pattern,
passed down to younger sister or cousin
and always
the bride wore yellow.
But Rosa's eyes grew ringed
in black waiting for her day,
the fabric of her youth stretching
to accommodate the years
that came and went
with the rejected suitors.
Each time she looked in the mirror,
there was more of herself she did not recognize.

Judith Ortiz Cofer

In night school English,
Rosa in her tight red dress
clashes with the green walls of a classroom
where day laborers carrying the day
on their faces, and women
wearing coats over housedresses
squeeze into desks meant for lighter bodies.
The professor lectures on subjects
as foreign to them
as their dark faces are to him.
He will not address this motley group
by their given names.
"Miss Malpaz," he calls on Rosa,
His pale blue eyes following a pattern
of pinpoint lights made by his gold watch
on the ceiling,
"Do you understand the meaning
of the line, 'My mistress' eyes
are nothing like the sun?'"
Rosa understands.
She knows the distance
between her and the man
who drops pretty words before them
like crumbs for the pigeons.
She understands.
So she pulls her eyes away
from the graven image
of his golden head,
sinking into her chair
in the posture of defeat
that they both understand.

Angels in Miami

Take the shape of dark children
waving white t-shirts
in a game of catch-me-if-you-can.
Old women stepping out
in white rubber shoes,
white as milk
under their umbrellas.
A rabbi in an evangelical rush
pedaling across the waves of traffic
on a bike ancient as the ark.
Medical students in white smocks
conducting their Lazarus debates
as they walk to lunch.
Sailboats swaying on the bay
like paper bells at a wedding.
A rush of feathers swooping down
into the water to pluck a fish,
flying it up like an offering to heaven.

The Angel of the Trash Collectors

In the twilight hours
between night and sunrise,
he travels in trucks laden
with the refuse of cities,
alongside men who leave their beds
at a dangerous time, the threads
of their unfinished dreams
trailing like exhaust behind them.
He hangs from a fender
dispelling the early morning fog
that clings to the road
with great sweeps of his grey wings.
He hovers just above their view
as they toss what's left of yesterday
into the vehicle's oblivious jaws.

My Brother's Son

for Alexander Miguel

Looks at us
with immense unfocused eyes
that seem to gaze within.
Called from the dark,
all he knows for now
are the little currents
that animate him
from foot to forehead.
In this slow turning to the light
is the moment when we all awakened.
We see ourselves
clinging to our mother's flesh,
and beyond the threshold of our bodies,
memories of tall grasses on a savanna,
the branches of a strong tree
twisted into muscled arms,
scented leaves for a nest;
our father's minted breath
as he tucked us in our beds,
the breath of a fire where we huddled
on the long nights of our origin,
and this child turning to find
the source of warmth
as I lean over his crib.
I whisper to him,
you have always been with us.

Judith Ortiz Cofer

Holly

for Tanya at eleven

Did I ever tell you holly doesn't grow
in that too hot place where I was born,
and that at your age
a grown-up kiss was forced on me
behind my grandmother's house
by a fourteen year old boy
I caught stealing her grapefruit?
Still green, he laughed,
and threw them at me.
For that waste I took the blame.
Both these facts you'd find hard to believe:
That Christmas can happen
without snow or bright lights,
and that a boy
would want to kiss your mother.
I'd like you to be innocent
of such a kiss
for a few more years, Tanya,
to have more days like the crisp,
cool morning
when you picked armfuls
of wild holly
at your grandmother's Georgia farm
under an iced sky,

nothing to distract you
but the rustling of dry leaves
as you made your way
deep into the woods.
Holly fills every container in my house.
I want to keep it green for you;
you want it dried to make wreaths—
its turning brown doesn't bother you,
you don't worry about the berries,
red as your cheeks that morning
when you gathered the branches,
that are now falling,
and as we crush them
with our winter boots,
they stain the floor like blood.

Judith Ortiz Cofer

Postcard Poem

It should be brief
and written in indelible ink,
so the postman's hands,
sweaty with the strain
of so many words on his shoulders,
will not smudge your message.
It should contain the expected,
wish you were here,
but no return address.
It should bear an exotic stamp
with the likeness of the martyred leader
of an underdeveloped nation, or a plea
to save a nearly extinct species
of sea mammal.
Through panoramic views
of impossibly blue skies
it should imply
that where you are
is the only place to be.

Glossary

Quinceañera—a girl, fifteen
San Antonio al Revés—San Antonio, upside down
       putas—whores
La Envidia—envy
La Fe—faith
La Maldad—evil
Loca—the mad woman
Las Malas Lenguas—the wagging tongues
       campesino—farmer
       maldita seas—may you be damned
       así dicen…—that's what the wagging tongues say
Siempre/Nunca—always/never
El Mal—evil
       Le hizo…—He cast evil on her
Costumbre—custom
Caminante—traveler
Esperanza—Hope
El Encanto—the spell
       y ni…magia—and not even the most powerful magic
La Bruja—the witch
Socorro—Succor (Our Lady of)
       flores…muertos—flowers for the dead
Día de los Muertos—the day of the dead (All Souls Day)
       campos—fields
Yerbatero—herbalist
       yerba…naturaleza—good herb, evil herb, / all is cured
              with faith / and nature
Estigmas—stigma(ta)
Cada Día—each day
       danos…día—give us our daily bread
       ruega por nosotros—pray for us
       Hijo…grande—Holy Son, of blue eyes and
              a great heart bleeding
Madrina—godmother
La Abuela—grandmother

Vestido de Novia—wedding dress
    boda—wedding
Matrimonio
    y yo…quizás—and I pray perhaps, perhaps
So much for Mañana
    el cura—the priest
Sueños—dreams
    mi pie…astros—my foot of sand and my head of stars
Acróbata—acrobat
    vamos…aplauda—Let's do dangerous stunts,
                modern acrobats,
                upon a trapeze of metaphors
                so the great public will applaud
Mamacita—mother dear
El Olvido—forgetfulness